"Today expect something good to happen to you no matter what o no longer holds you captive. It can only continue to hurt you if you nota on to u. let the past go. A simply abundant world awaits."— Sarah Breathnach

People with an abundant mindset see the world in terms of win-win. They are genuinely happy for the successes, well-being, achievements, recognition and good fortune of other people.

They go out of their way to help others and contribute to their greatness because in doing so they believe we can all achieve more.

People with an abundant mindset also operate from a strong sense of self-worth. They know the results they see (or don't see) in their lives are a direct representation of how they feel about themselves.

They believe that if they want to transform their dreams into reality and create lives they love living, it's important to see themselves as someone who is 100% WORTHY of living their dream life — and capable of creating it.

Consequently, they're able to generate new opportunities and possibilities for themselves and their lives much more easily than others may be able to.

To shift yourself into an abundant mindset, you must first embrace the truth that we live in a truly abundant world and infinite intelligence has countless ways to bless you. It may not always feel this way when you're experiencing scarcity, lack or a setback, but it's true.

If your bank account balance is low, you might have a feeling of lack, but if you suddenly receive a large bonus at work, you may start thinking of yourself as abundant...

The reason that you probably don't have money is because you're desperate. Understand what I'm saying here. If you're desperate for it, you're not going to manifest it. Why? Because the law of attraction says that like energy attracts like energy. What is money? Money is just energy. This physical world isn't even physical. It's just energy.

What are your thoughts? Your thoughts are nonphysical energy. You can't see your thoughts, but they're energy that's vibrating outside of the speed of light that your eyes can perceive. When you desperately need money, what energy are you in? You're in an energy of lack.

What does lack create? More lack. You make the wrong decision to go into business with the wrong person because you're desperate and hoping that you can make money. You, you do things that you wouldn't normally do and you think of ways that aren't positive and abundant so you attract situations and experiences.

How Wanting Something Too Much Can Block Receiving

How Wanting Something Too Much Can Block Receiving

There may have been times when you desperately wanted something so much, but these wants and actions did not produce positive results. You might have put everything in place in a practical sense in order to help you receive, yet nothing came from your efforts.

While it's true that there are occasions when the things you want cannot come into your life because it's the wrong time for them to appear or the universe has other ideas for you, often, the main reason that you don't get what you want is due to resistance.

Resistance comes in the form of inherited lies that play constantly in your subconscious. I will share with you a few to get the drift that this tape in your head that is playing these "infalicies" is lying to you and will stop your abundance mindset.

Lie #1 Losing body parts builds wealth
Now your parents might not have phrased it that way, but if you ever put your tooth under a pillow and waited for the Tooth Fairy to bring you a buck, then you know this one.

Thankfully, most 5-year-olds aren't ready to begin following the logic here. If they did, they might start wondering, How much can I get for an ear?

Lie #2 Everyone's a winner
This one might have come from your Little League coach, or maybe your parents passed it along in some way. It's the idea that winners and losers don't exist—that everyone gets a trophy, everyone deserves equal playing time, and keeping score is somehow immoral.

Here's my thoughts on that: Nah. If you want to raise an entitled kid, teach him that he deserves to win—to get paid as much as everyone else—just by showing up. Then see how well his employer reacts to that in 20 years.

Lie # 3 Lying Can Instill Fear in Children
I developed an unhealthy relationship with money because of what I saw my mother go through. I made saving a priority, but I had a hard time

bringing myself to spend any money. I was fearful of what would happen if I did.

This came as a direct result of witnessing what happened to my mother who wasn't a saver. She was deep in debt and couldn't save because at the end of the day, all of her money was allocated toward bills.

When anything major happened, such as the fridge not working, or the washing machine shutting down, she had to put it on credit. This meant going further into debt, and added more stress to the situation.

Always wanting to spend the least amount possible and constantly depriving myself wasn't very healthy. Only in the last few years have I managed to be more laid back about my spending. I'm still financially responsible, of course, but I don't agonize over pennies

There are so many more lies that we were told in our youth and things that we saw financially that indelibly imprinted on how we feel about money. Today I am challenging you to end that tape playing in the back of your mind and give way to the way we were intended to believe.

Those that choose to walk along the path of abundance experience a completely different life.

Opting to live life to the fullest, exuding happiness, generous by nature, creative and inspirational. Taking full advantage and enjoying the wave of opportunities that come their way, along with memorable experiences.

The secret to having it all is believing you already do.

Scarcity vs. Abundance Mindset

There is a major difference between those with a scarcity mindset vs an abundance mindset. A person with an **abundance** mindset believes that there **is** always more **of** everything in life, whether that's money, relationships, resources, opportunities, etc. Alternatively, someone **with a scarcity** mentality lives in fear that they are going to lose their time or money. Let's delve into the verses theory of the haves and the have nots.

1. Thinking Big vs Thinking Small

Those with an abundant mindset are renowned for thinking big, it is part of their DNA. Scarcity mindset creates limitations in the mind which prevents the creation of bold goals.

2. Plenty vs Lack

Those with an abundance mentality believe there is plenty of everything in the world from resources, love, relationships, wealth and opportunities. They believe they can afford what they want in life and say exactly that : 'I can afford that...'

Those with a lack mentality prefer to believe that there are limited opportunities, resources, relationships, love and wealth. They consistently say: 'I cannot afford that...'. I am broke. I don't have ... Saying those statements every day reinforces the belief and forms that exact pattern in the life as reality.

The scarcity trap captures this notion we see again and again in many domains. When people have very little, they undertake behaviors that maintain or reinforce their future disadvantage. If you have very little, you often behave in such a way so that you'll have little in the future. -Sendhil Mullainathan

3. Happiness vs Resentment

Someone with an abundant mentality is an optimist and is genuinely happy for others when they achieve success. Conversely, those with a scarcity mindset are competitive and resent others success.

4. Embracing Change vs Fear Of Change

A person with an abundant mindset understands that change is an integral part of life, They embrace and accept change. Appreciating the fact that change often leads to more positive outcomes, even if change is somewhat challenging or difficult to navigate.

Fear plagues those with a scarcity mindset. They will spend time constantly complaining along about change and take a longer period of time to accept change.

5. Proactive vs Reactive

Due to the positive attitude of those with an abundant mindset, they take a proactive approach to life.

Rather than waiting for things to happen and then reacting like those with a scarcity mindset do, they strategically plan for the future and create strategies for the long-term.

6. Learning vs Knowing It All

An abundance mentality craves learning and growth. They have a never ending thirst for knowledge and developing new skills whereas scarcity mindset believe they know everything thereby severely limiting their learning and growth.

7. What Is Working vs What Is Not Working

A person with a scarcity mindset selects negative thoughts and adopts a victim mentality.

The strong emotions they experience on a daily basis creates stress in the body with the range of emotions shifting from anxiety, fear, worry, anger and resentment. Their negative emotions, thoughts and beliefs create illnesses in the body leading to general poor health. Their daily focus is on 'What is not working'.

Those with an abundance mindset are often visionaries and see the limitless possibilities in the world. Their focus in daily life is on 'What is working'.

The path you have traveled this far is not set in stone, such is the beauty of life you can change. Deciding to change paths is the first step.

Life is short, live large, believe in the endless possibilities life has to offer and choose to live an abundant life creating memorable moments you can cherish forever.

There's an old saying that says "Be careful what you wish for--you may get it!" Well, most people get exactly what they wish for. They get what they are anticipating.

Anticipation is like a deep, inner wish--a looking forward with expectations good or bad. We have to learn that wishes are nothing but our desire to see things clearly from our perspective. So if we are abundant thinkers we will not look for presumptuous of a bad outcome, but of one that encapsulates the goodness that you want for yourself and others. Change your mind yet?

Sabotage

For some reason, people sabotage their own success by wallowing around in the muddy waters of their own worst expectations in what we call a "pity party" saying things like

I'll never make it

I'm too old

They don't want me

Success is for others--not for me

I don't have what it takes

It'll never fly

If you think like this, you are anticipating, you are almost wishing for that very outcome, and the universe, like a genie in a bottle, will grant you your wish and give you what you are anticipating.

The universe is made up of energy, and if you are creating this kind of negative, defeatist energy around yourself, you will experience exactly that. What you should be doing is setting yourself up to anticipate the success that is coming to you. Anticipate winning. Anticipate finding methods to success. Anticipate succeeding, and you will have the strength and the positive energy to go ahead and succeed! It isn't magic. It's logic.

Any time you say, I can't do it; it's hopeless, it becomes hopeless and you won't be able to do it, because you are so numbed by despair and a "give up" spirit. So arm yourself with the mental tool of anticipating success. Do you feel that positive stimulation when you anticipate success? Why shouldn't success come to you? A universe of abundance is waiting to bestow its gifts on you.

Anticipating success energizes you to take positive action toward its achievement. After all, why do anything at all if you don't think you will succeed at it? Why get up in the morning? Because you have to? Because you are alive? No, because you anticipate that today will bring some things worth having. Today will bring some success, and success is worth making an effort toward.

If you anticipate success, you will make that phone call, send that email, postthat blog, approach that person, attend a networking event, set up that interview, make that sale, or write that contract in favorable terms. Why? Because it's going to turn out well! You are charged up to take effective action when you anticipate success, and your efforts will be rewarded. You will attract success like a magnet.

Deep inside, many of us have a fear of failure, so we fail to try. We fulfill our own negative prophecy. Or we do things half-heartedly because we are listening to those cancerous old thoughts of fearing what might happen, thinking, but what if such and such happens? What if? What if? when we think like that, we sabotage our own efforts at success.

Most people who set New Year's resolutions, less than 10% actually achieve them. Bby thinking, what if? and fearing the worst, you're actually sending out a message to the universe that you want the worst to happen, because it's the foremost thought in your mind. So what's the solution? Simple. Keep success at the forefront of your mind and tell the universe you expect nothing but success.

Sometimes we fearfully repeat the same old actions that have brought the same old results because at least we know what will happen then--the same
old failure! Once we begin to anticipate success, though, there is no reason not to change things up a bit and do things differently and with enthusiasm. Why not experiment when success is going to be the outcome? Why not take a little risk? Why not step off the beaten path just a little? Success lies ahead, so we can take those chances and, as the old saying goes, "Nothing ventured, nothing gained."

When we zero in on negative expectations, usually based on bad experiences from the past, they have a way of coming true. Instead of zeroing in on the past like a homing device, let's look forward to a future of success, expecting the best. Why not? People who are more successful than you are not smarter, better, superior, wiser, grander, or any different than you are. The main difference is that their minds are set to attract success, and yours hasn't been. Until now!

Ask, Believe and be

Prepared to Receive

Ask, Believe and be Prepared to Receive

Since you are going to get what you wish for, and you are beginning to anticipate success, you need to be ready to receive it when it comes. W

They did not know how to be wealthy, so they lost their wealth. Many of them went bankrupt after winning millions of dollars--or wound up back in the same old beat-up, run-down trailer they started out from! They weren't ready to receive or manage their wealth, so it left them right back where they started from.

You must learn to receive wealth by learning how wealth is accumulated. Knowledge is power. For example, Albert Einstein said that compound interest was a miracle! Learn to put the miracle of compound interest to work by building up an account that earns high interest. Don't touch the main amount (the principal) and keep reinvesting the interest. Let it snowball. Money making money is a beautiful thing!

Another way to receive wealth is by investing. Investments make money. It is worth your while to study investments. Read about the stock market. Learn about stocks and bonds. Talk to stock brokerage and financial management firms. Look at your assets and begin to figure out ways to leverage them so that they are building wealth for you. If you don't have a lot of money to invest at first, investigate penny stocks or micro-financing. There are opportunities to invest on many levels.

The simplest way to build up money is to pay out less than you take in. That way you will have some left over to invest and save. Live within your income, and use any extra to invest. Through making a budget, figure out ways to increase your income and decrease your expenses, and you will have extra money to plug into investments and savings.

Saving is another important way to prepare to receive wealth. Savings show
the universe that you have self-control when it comes to money, and more money will then naturally gravitate toward you. Savings can serve as a cushion in case things go wrong; some of those savings can be invested so that they are earning money for you; other savings can go toward worthy causes and/or be used to accrue interest.
Even without interest, savings tend to multiply. It is as if money attracts more money, or the universe recognizes your desire to have money because you are saving. Even if you can only add a little to your savings at a time, you will be surprised at how quickly your fund will grow. You will also start noticing new opportunities to save--the bonus at work, the birthday gift money, the inheritance, the auto repair that was less than the amount you budgeted for, thus leaving you with some extra to plug into savings--

opportunities to put money away will crop up once you have made it clear that you want to save.

When I studied Suze Ormann money course she stated, money comes to those who respect it. One of the most respectful things you can do is to start investing and saving, which I did right away, of course. When you begin to see money as something that you need to respect and put to work for good causes, like a proper retirement or your children's education, money will gravitate toward you because you are its respectful keeper, a good steward. You can put away tidy sums in a well-ordered way and show yourself to be a person who can be trusted with wealth.

Learn business strategies to help you be more effective at work or at your own business and to generate more money. Learn from shows like "Shark Tank" or other entrepreneur/small business shows on television. Read business and investment magazines. Read about rich people and how they succeeded. Study their lives, words, attitudes, and advice. Start mentally hanging around with them to develop a wealthy mindset. Learn, learn, learn.

Pay attention to your mind. They say everyone has at least three ideas for a
new business every day; we are just not aware of them. As our minds are idle, flipping through the refrigerator looking for a snack, we sometimes get a blinding inspiration about a new product, process, or business.

Your ideas are your treasure trove too, so write them down. They're worth saving! Some of them may be worth acting upon.
Again, money and good fortune comes to those who are ready to receive them and use them well. Show money that you are ready to receive, and respect it by treating what wealth you have in wise, sane, well-ordered, and

sensible ways. Create some opportunities for money to come to you to be used wisely and respectfully, and more of it will come to you.

The universe knows when you're ready to receive money in your life. By focusing your thoughts on what you desire, the universe will deliver. You just have to know how to tell the universe you're ready to receive the wealth that

Do Some Work

Here are some questions you need to ask yourself before you get into the next chapter.

You Need to Know What You Really Want

Take a moment to reflect honestly on the following questions:

- ☐ What does success look like for me?
- ☐ What areas of my life need ramping up or outright transformation?
- ☐ What steps do I need to take in those areas to move toward the success I envision?
- ☐ What does my heart tells me I should do?
- ☐ What would a big break look like in my life?
- ☐ How can I jump start that big break taking place?

Here's some work you need to do after things happen:

- ☐ Sit down and think about serious problems you have had in the past which is now over. Write down the good habits, insights, practices, or character strengths that came out of it
- ☐ Write down your current biggest "problem". Now adjust your perspective.
- ☐ What are some good habits, insights, practices, or character strengths that could come out of coping with it? What can you learn from it?
- ☐ Accept that life involves a certain amount of setbacks. Life will throw you curveballs. It's what you do with them that will determine your ultimate reward.
- ☐ Accept that adversity is there to teach you, not to torment you.

⬚ Post a list of problems overcome in your life to serve as a source of strength when the going gets rough.

Things Happen It's Not a Punishment

Sometimes it happens. Something goes horribly wrong. A relationship you treasured has become toxic or has even broken off. No matter how hard you fought to stay creditworthy, debt overwhelmed you. The child you doted on grew up to be defiant. Your new exercise machine produced a damaged nerve in your back. Your new product just isn't selling. Someone you loved has died. Your business partner betrayed you. The office was broken into and irreplaceable records lost.

All of us will experience some pain, suffering, disappointment, and loss in our lives. Such things are inevitable. Yet many of us believe that when bad things happen to us, we are being punished for past misdeeds or shortcomings.

Yes it's true, we attract what we focus on. Yes it's true, our destinies are, to a large extent, in our own hands.

Yet circumstances happen too; other people have free will and they make choices we have no control over. You might have had little to do with the problem you are facing.

Surely all the people who suffered losses during Superstorm Sandy or the great and terrible tsunami years back did not bring that upon themselves. Don't shoulder all the blame for the storms that are hitting your life either. It is especially important not to think that because bad things are happening to you, you should dissolve into self-doubt and uncertainty, beating yourself up because you think you are undeserving of anything but strife. You should not think the universe has turned against you, or that you are a losing pawn in some cosmic chess game.

Not at all. In fact, sometimes adversity is just the universe's way of getting your attention so you can learn important life lessons that will propel you to success once you have overcome it. The universe wants to give you success because you deserve it; there might be a few things in the way.

Nature loathes a vacuum. If there is an empty place, it will be filled, just as wind is a rush of air to fill an empty space.

When you go through suffering, a lot gets emptied out: misdirected wishes, vain imaginings, misunderstandings about yourself and others, wrong directions. When you are suffering, what is really important becomes crystal clear.

As you empty yourself out through suffering, there is room for something new and wonderful to come in. This is the way the universe works to bring abundance into your life.

Adversity also forces you to fight, so it builds up your mental and emotional muscles. One man learned to swim because his big brother and friends tossed him into a lake! It was sink or swim! While we don't endorse this method of teaching someone how to swim, it does illustrate the point that sometimes difficulty makes you into the fighter and survivor you would otherwise not have been.

The adaptations you learn through coping with adversity will help you not only survive but flourish. It helps you evolve into a bigger and better person with greater "emotional intelligence" and life skills.

Shakespeare said "sweet are the uses of adversity." That means adversity can sometimes turn out to be a good thing--or at least good can result from it.

Overcoming adversity strengthens you so you can take on more responsibility and the bigger blessings that go with that.

Adversity is a great teacher. That's what it's there for. It's not the rod of the universe's anger beating you down. It's there to show you that you might be on the wrong path; it's a way marker. It's a sign that you might need to revise your current approach to success or to try new approaches. It is always there to teach you, not to torment you.

I am here to tell you that the "grit" attained through overcoming failure is a character quality that can see a person through to success in life. In fact, building resilience through picking up the pieces and soldiering on after a failure will definitely lead to success.

Being able to bounce back after a setback, being able to keep trying when everything around you seems dark and hopeless--those are character strengths or virtues that can steer you to success in the long run. When you face difficulties, know that the universe is preparing you for greatness, because no one becomes super successful without the qualities of resilience and persistence that adversity hones in a person's character.

I hope you now have a better understanding of what it takes to live a life of abundance. While the universe plays a part in granting your desires, it all begins with you. Your thoughts are the driving force of what the universe eventually manifests into your life. What you keep at the forefront of your mind is what you're actually asking the universe for.

Reasons to Be Wealthy

Why is it that people don't become wealthy?
First, and foremost they do not believe it can be them.

The average person has grown up in a family where he has never met or known anyone who was wealthy. She goes to school and socializes with people who are not wealthy. She works with people who are not wealthy. She has a *reference group* or a social circle outside of work who are not wealthy. She has no role models who are wealthy. If this has happened to you throughout your formative years, up to the age of twenty, you can grow up and become a fully mature adult in our society, and it may never occur to you that it's just as possible for you to become wealthy as for anyone else.

So the first reason why people don't become wealthy is it never occurs to them that it is possible for them. And of course, if it never occurs to them, then they never take any of the steps necessary to make it a reality.

They Never Make A Decision

The second reason that people don't become wealthy is that they never decide to.

Even if a person reads a book, attends a lecture, or associate with people who are financially successful, nothing changes until she makes a decision to do something different. Even if it occurs to a person that she could become wealthy if she just did certain things in a specific way, if she doesn't decide to take the first step, she ends up staying as she is.

If you continue to do what you've always done, you'll continue to get what you've always got.

The primary reason for underachievement and failure is that the great majority of people don't decide to be successful. They never make a firm, unequivocal commitment or definite decision that they are going to become wealthy. They mean to, and they intend to, and they hope to and they're going to, *someday.* They wish and hope and pray that they will make a lot of money, but they never decide, "I am going to do it!" This decision is an essential first step to becoming financially independent.

Putting It Off

The third reason that people don't become abundant is *procrastination*.

People always have a good reason not to begin doing what they know they need to do to achieve financial independence. It is always the wrong month, the wrong season, or the wrong year. Business conditions in their industry are no good, or they may be too good or they are just not in the mood. The market isn't right. They may have to take a risk, or give up their security. Maybe next year.

There always seems to be a reason to procrastinate. As a result, they keep putting it off, month by month, year by year, until it's too late. Even if it has occurred to a person that they can become wealthy, and they have made a decision to change, procrastination will push all their plans into the indefinite future.

Pay The Price

The fourth reason that people retire poor is what economists call the *inability to delay gratification.*

The great majority of people have an irresistible temptation to spend every single penny they make and whatever else they can borrow or buy on credit. If you cannot delay gratification, and discipline yourself to refrain from spending everything you make, you cannot become abundant. If you cannot practice budgeting as a lifelong habit, it will be impossible for you to achieve financial independence.

"It's unfortunate how some people complain about being financially unstable, yet they use their last savings to acquire material things." — Edmond Mbiaka

Take The Long View

The fifth reason that people transition to not working are poor is more important than all the others is *lack of time perspective*.

In a longitudinal study conducted by Dr. Edward Banfield at Harvard University in the 1950s and published in 1964 as *The Unheavenly City*, he studied the reasons for upward socio-economic mobility. He wanted to know how you could predict whether an individual or a family was going to move upward one or more socio-economic groupings and be wealthier in the next generation than they were this generation.

All his research brought him to a single factor that he concluded was more accurate than any other in predicting success in America. They called it *time* perspective. This was defined as the amount of time that you take into consideration when planning your day-to-day activities and when making important decisions in your life. Time perspective refers to how far you projected into the future when you decided what you were going to do or not do in the present.

A young couple that begins putting $50 dollars a month aside in a scholarship fund so that their newborn child can go to the college or university of his or her choice is a couple with a long time perspective. They are willing to sacrifice in the short term to assure better results and outcomes in the long term. People with long time perspective almost always move up economically in the course of their lifetimes.

I know that you read that I threw wealth into the abundance mindset, it is because they are so closely related in our perception. But they are different and yield different results.

Abundance throws a wider net over a whole host of life areas; all of which can be instrumental in our very greatest happiness. An abundant love life, an abundance of good health, an abundant career, social life, an abundance of peace or achievements; it is abundance in life areas such as these that can make us truly 'wealthy'. This is the case, both spiritually and physically!

When we strive to achieve great wealth, in the form of money only, we limit ourselves and our happiness greatly. Wealth can be a wonderful thing, but it counts for only one single aspect of our lives. It does not guarantee good health, fulfilling relationships or levels of achievement that great happiness can stem from. When we forever chase money, remaining focused solely on our bank balance; we begin to feel very poor indeed. The bigger picture is lost to us.

It is, however, still possible to manifest money and wealth while still being happy. But really think about what makes you *truly* happy before you start making any risky decisions.

The Real Difference Between Wealth And Abundance

"We are buried beneath the weight of information, which is being confused with knowledge; quantity is being confused with abundance and wealth with happiness."– Tom Waits

When we choose to strive for abundance as opposed to wealth, we are presented with the exciting possibility of becoming 'better off' in every aspect of our lives. Including money!

The difference between making money through an 'abundant' mindset as opposed to a wealthy one is that money can come as a result of the abundance you create in the rest of your life.

Basically, why stick to chasing one dream, when that dream can come true while you are chasing many others?

Sound Too Good To Be True?

Well, for the majority of people it is! This is why so few of us are able to drop our dreams for money and replace it with a dream of lifelong abundance. We are so busy chasing the 'golden nugget' of wealth that we become blind to the abundance that we have failed to create in other areas of our life.

Chasing riches can be a worthwhile pursuit as long as it is part of your bigger, lifelong picture. For example, if you were to become rich beyond your wildest dreams, what would you do with the money? Money without an abundance of passion or purpose can only result in restlessness and a ceaseless thirst for more. An abundant life, however, can help to transform your life into the ideal vessel for attracting money and using it as a welcome addition to your already happy, fulfilled life.

When you pursue money only, you will always feel as though you never have enough. This is when you are so fixated on getting rich that you can only ever feel emotions of 'want' and 'lack' concerning money; preventing you from ever really achieving financial abundance.

Why race through life in tireless pursuit of something that you feel is forever out of your reach? Or would you rather invest your emotions and energies into the things that bring you infinite abundance and lasting joy?

Connection, not competition. Truth, not things. Fulfillment, not a career. Abundance not wealth. That is where true happiness and the very greatest riches in life can be uncovered.

Printed in Great Britain
by Amazon

25694276R00020